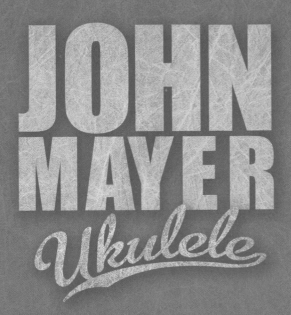

CONTENTS

Cover photo by Albert Watson

Cherry Lane Music Company
Director of Publications/Project Editor: Mark Phillips

ISBN: 978-1-60378-383-5

Visit our website at www.cherrylaneprint.com

Back to You

Words and Music by
John Mayer

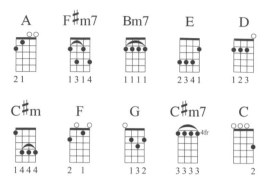

Intro   A | |F#m7 | |Bm7 |E |F#m7 |

Verse 1

A | |
   Back to you.   It always comes around.
F#m7 | |Bm7
   Back to you.   I tried to forget   you,
            |E
I tried to stay away,
       |F#m7 | |
But it's too   late.

A | |
   Over you,   I'm never over,
F#m7 | |Bm7
   Over you.   There's something about   you,
           |E
It's just the way you move,
       |F#m7 | ||
The way you   move me.

Chorus 1

```
         E           |F#m7   D           |
Yeah, I'm so good at forgetting,
         E           |F#m7 D        |E
   And I quit every game I play.
              |F#m7 C#m  D      |
But for - give  me,  love.
              Bm7                   |E                ||
I can't turn and walk away      this  way.
```

Interlude 1

```
         A         |       |F#m7   |       |Bm7     |E      |F#m7     |       ||
```

Verse 2

```
         A                |                        |
   Back to you.     It always comes around.
F#m7              |                    |Bm7
   Back to you.      I walk with your shad - ow,
                          |E
I'm sleeping in my bed
              |F#m7 |        ||
With your silhou - ette.
```

Chorus 2

```
         E           |F#m7        D      |
Yeah, should have smiled in that picture,
         E           |F#m7      D      |E
   If it's the last thing I'll see of you.
         |F#m7 C#m  D      |
It's the least  that  you
         Bm7       |E             ||
Could   not do.
```

Bridge

```
      E        |F       |G        |
      Ah.

      E        A        |D
        Leave  the light    on,
       |E        A       |D          |
      I'll never give up  on you.
      E        A        |D         |Bm7        |
        Leave  the light    on,  for me,     too,
             |C♯m7       |        |C      |D           ||
      For me,        too,   for me,   too.      Yeah.
```

Interlude 2   A | |F♯m7 | |Bm7 |E |F♯m7 | ||

Outro

```
      A                |                |
        Back to me,    I know that it comes
      F♯m7             |                |Bm7
        Back to me.    Doesn't it scare    you?
                            |E
      Your will is not as strong
         |F♯m7            |         ||
      As it    used to be.
```

Bigger Than My Body

Words and Music by
John Mayer

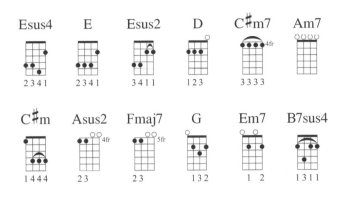

Intro

Esus4 | E | Esus4 | E |

Esus4 | E | Esus4 | E ||

Verse 1

Esus4 | E |
This is a call to the col - or blind.

Esus2 | E
This is an IOU.

| Esus4 | E
I'm stranded behind the hori - zon line,

| Esus4 | E ||
Tied   up in something true.

Pre-Chorus 1

E | D |
    Yes, I'm grounded,   got my wings clipped.

C#m7 | Am7 |
    I'm surrounded by   all this pavement.

E | D |
    Guess I'll circle   while I'm waiting

Am7 | |
For my fuse to dry.

Chorus 1

‖C♯m |E |Asus2 |

Someday I'll fly,   someday   I'll soar.

       |C♯m |E |Asus2 |

Someday I'll be   so damn   much more,

     |C♯m |E |Asus2 | ‖

'Cause I'm bigger than my bod - y gives me cred - it for.

Verse 2

Esus4 |E |

     Why is it not the time?

Esus2 |E |

What is there more to learn?

Esus4 |E |

    Shed this skin   I've been tripping in,

Esus4 |E   ‖

Never to quite return.

Repeat Pre-Chorus 1

Chorus 2

‖C♯m |E |Asus2 |

Someday I'll fly,   someday   I'll soar.

    |C♯m |E |Asus2 |

Someday I'll be   so damn   much more,

   |C♯m |E |Asus2 |

'Cause I'm bigger than my bod - y gives me cred - it for.

   |C♯m |E |D | ‖

'Cause I'm bigger than my bod - y now.

Interlude   C♯m |E |Asus2 | |C♯m |E |Asus2 | ‖

Bridge

Fmaj7 G |Em7   Fmaj7 | G |Em7   Fmaj7
May - be I'll tangle in   the pow - er lines.

      |Fmaj7 G |Em7 Fmaj7 | G |Em7   Fmaj7
And it might be   over in   a sec - ond's time.

       |Fmaj7   G |Em7   Fmaj7
But I'll glad - ly   go down in a flame

        |F♯m7 |B7sus4
If a flame's   what it takes to remem - ber my name,

       |B7sus4 ||
To remem - ber my name, yeah.

Pre-Chorus 2

E |D |
  Yes, I'm grounded,   got my wings clipped.

C♯m7 |Am7 |
   I'm surrounded by   all this pavement.

E |D |
  Guess I'll circle   while I'm waiting

Am7 |
For my fuse to dry. (For my fuse to dry.)

   |Am7 |
Wait   for my fuse to dry.

Chorus 3

|| C#m | E | Asus2 |
Someday I'll fly,   someday   I'll soar.

|C#m | E | Asus2 |
Someday I'll be   so damn   much more,

|C#m | E
'Cause I'm bigger than my bod - y.

|Asus2 |
I'm bigger than my bod - y.

|B7sus4 | |
I'm bigger than my bod - y now.

Esus4 | E | Esus4 | E ||

Outro

B7sus4 | | E | Esus4 |
Oh,   ooh,   oh.

B7sus4 | | E | |
Oh,   ooh,   oh.

B7sus4 | | E | Esus4 |
Oh,   ooh,   oh.

B7sus4 | | E | ||
Oh,   ooh,   oh.

Clarity

Words and Music by
John Mayer

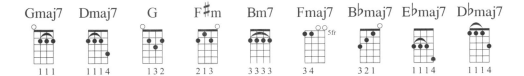

Intro

|Gmaj7 |Dmaj7 |Gmaj7 |Dmaj7|

Verse 1

           ‖**Gmaj7** |**Dmaj7**
I wor   -   ry I weigh three times my body.

        |**Gmaj7** |**Dmaj7**
I wor   -   ry I throw my fear a - round.

          |**Gmaj7** |**Dmaj7** |
But this morning there's a calm   I can't explain.

Gmaj7 |**Dmaj7**
      The rock candy's melted, only dia - monds now remain.

  |**Gmaj7** |**Dmaj7** |**Gmaj7** |**Dmaj7**
Ooh,   ooh,   ooh,   ooh

Verse 2

           ‖**Gmaj7** |**Dmaj7**
By the time I recognize this   moment,

        |**Gmaj7** |**Dmaj7**
This moment will be gone.

          |**Gmaj7** |**Dmaj7**
But I will bend the light, pretending

          |**Gmaj7** |**Dmaj7**
That it somehow lingered on.

                        |**Gmaj7** |**Dmaj7** |**Gmaj7** |**Dmaj7**   ‖
When all I got's... Ooh,   ooh,   ooh,   ooh.

Chorus 1

```
      G     F#m  Bm7|              |
                  And I will wait to find
      G     F#m  Bm7|              |
                  If this will last forever.
      G     F#m  Bm7|              |
                  And I will wait to find
      G     F#m  Bm7|              |
                  If this will last forever.
      G     F#m  Bm7|              |
                  And I will pay no mind
      G     F#m       Bm7|
              When it      won't, and it won't
              |Gmaj7           |Dmaj7
Because it        can't,  it just      can't.
              |Gmaj7           |Dmaj7
It's not supposed       to.
```

Verse 3

```
              ||Gmaj7                           |Dmaj7
Was there a second of time that I looked around?
          |Gmaj7                               |Dmaj7
Did I      sail through or drop my anchor down?
         |Gmaj7                      |Dmaj7
Was anything enough to kiss the ground
                   |Gmaj7           |Dmaj7
And say I'm here now? And she's here now.
         |Gmaj7    |Dmaj7     |Gmaj7      |Dmaj7
Ooh,        ooh,        ooh,        ooh.
         |Gmaj7    |Dmaj7     |Gmaj7      |Dmaj7    ||
Ooh,        ooh,        ooh,        ooh.
```

Interlude   Fmaj7 |B♭maj7 |E♭maj7 | ||

Bridge

Fmaj7	|B♭maj7	|E♭maj7			

So much wast - ed in the af - ternoon.

Fmaj7	|B♭maj7	|E♭maj7		

So much sa - cred in the month of June.

|D♭maj7 | | |Dmaj7 | |Gmaj7 | ‖

How 'bout you? Uh.

Chorus 2

G   F♯m Bm7|

And I will wait to find

G   F♯m Bm7|

If this will last forever.

G   F♯m Bm7|

And I will wait to find

G   F♯m   Bm7|

That it won't and it won't, and it won't.

G   F♯m Bm7|

And I won't pay no mind

G   F♯m Bm7|

Worried 'bout no rainy weather.

G   F♯m Bm7|

And I will waste no time

G   F♯m   Bm7 |

Re - main - ing in our lives together.

G   F♯m   Bm7 |

Vocal ad lib (till end)

G   F♯m   Bm7 |

G   F♯m   Bm7 | ‖

Come Back to Bed

Words and Music by
John Mayer

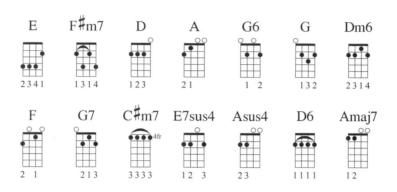

Intro   E |F#m7   D |E |F#m7   D ||

Verse 1

A |G6   G |
Still is the life

D |Dm6 |
Of your room when you're not inside.

A |G6   G |
And all of your things

D |F   G7 |
Tell the sweetest story line.

A |G |
Your tears on these sheets

D |Dm6 |
And your footsteps are down the hall.

A |G
So tell me what I   did.

|D |E |
I can't find where the moment went wrong at all.

Pre-Chorus 1

‖F♯m7   D   │E

You can be mad in the morn - ing.

|F♯m7   D   │E

I'll take back what I said.

|F♯m7   C♯m7   │D

Just don't leave   me a - lone here. It's cold, baby.

Chorus 1

E7sus4   ‖Asus4 A   │D6

Come back to bed,

D   │Asus4 A   │D6

Come back to bed,

D   │Asus4 A   │D6

Come back to bed,

D   │Asus4 A

Come back to bed,

|Dm6   ‖

Come on back to bed.

Verse 2

A   │G6 G   │

What will this fix?

D   │Dm6   │

You know you're not a quick forgive.

A   │G

And I won't sleep through this.

|D   │E   │

I survive   on the breath you are finished with.

Repeat Pre-Chorus 1

Chorus 2

```
E7sus4        ‖Asus4  A        |D6
```
Come back to bed,
```
D             |Asus4  A        |D6
```
Come back to bed,
```
D             |Asus4  A        |D6
```
Come back to bed,
```
D             |Asus4  A        |D        |E          |
```
Come back to bed.

Pre-Chorus 2

```
         ‖F♯m7              D      |E
```
You can be mad in the morn - ing
```
      |F♯m7            D     |E
```
Or the afternoon instead.
```
           |F♯m7                    C♯m7              |D
```
But don't leave me ninety eight and six de - grees of separation from you, baby.

Chorus 3

```
E7sus4        ‖Asus4  A        |D6
```
Come back to bed,
```
D             |Asus4  A        |D6
```
Come back to bed,
```
D             |Asus4  A        |
```
Come back to bed.
```
D6                D             |Asus4  A        |D6      D
```
Why don't you come back to bed?

Outro

      ‖**A** |**D**
Don't hold your love over my head.

      |**A** |**D**
Don't hold your love over my head.

      |**A** |**D**
Don't hold your love over my head.

      |**A** |**D**
Don't hold your love over my head.

      |**A**   **Amaj7** |**D6**
Don't hold your love over my head.

      |**A**   **Amaj7**|**D6**   ‖
Don't hold your love...

Comfortable

Words and Music by
John Mayer and Clay Cook

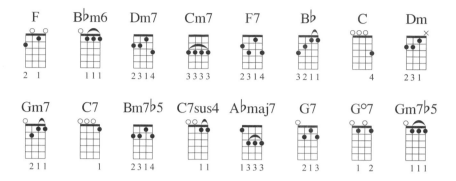

Intro

F |B♭m6 |Dm7 |Cm7 F7 |

B♭ |C   Dm |Gm7 |C   Dm   ‖

Verse 1

F |B♭m6 |
I just remembered that time at the market;

Dm7 |Cm7   F7 |B♭
Snuck up behind me and jumped on my shopping cart

   |C   Dm |Gm7 |C   Dm |
And rode down   Aisle Five.

F |B♭m6 |
You looked behind you to smile back at me,

Dm7 |Cm7   F7 |B♭
Crashed into a rack full of maga - zines.

   |C   Dm |Gm7|C   Dm |F |B♭m6 |Dm7 |F7   ‖
They asked us   if we could leave.

Pre-Chorus 1

B♭　　|C7　　　　　|B♭　　　　　|C7
Can't re - member what went wrong last Sep - tember,
　　　　　　　　|B♭　　　　　|C7　　　　|Bm7♭5　　　|　　　　　　||
Though I'm sure that you'd re - mind me if you had to.

Chorus

F　　|　　　|Dm7　　|　　　|
　　Our love was　　comfort - 'ble and
B♭　|　　|C7sus4 |C7
　　So broken in.

Verse 2

||F　　　　　　　　　|B♭m6
I sleep with this new girl I'm still getting used to.
　|Dm7　　　　　　　|Cm7　　F7　|B♭
My friends all approve, say, "She's gonna be good for you."
　　|C　　Dm|Gm7　|C　　Dm　|
They throw me　　high fives.
Γ　　　　　　|D♭m6　　　|
She says the Bible is all that she reads
Dm7　　　　　|Cm7　　　F7　|B♭
　And prefers that I not use pro - fani - ty.
　|C　　Dm |Gm7 |C　　Dm ||
Your mouth was　　so dirt - y.

Pre-Chorus 2

B♭　　|C7　　　|B♭　　　|C7
Life of the party, and she swears that she's artsy,
　|B♭　　　|C7　　　|Bm7♭5　　|　　　　||
But you could dis - tinguish Miles from Coltrane.

17

Chorus 2

F | |Dm7 | |
   Our love was   comfort - 'ble and

B♭ | |C7sus4 |C7 |
   So broken in.

F | |Dm7 | |
   She's perfect,   so flawless,

A♭maj7 |Cm7 |Dm7 |G7 |B♭ |G°7 |
    Or so they say.   Hey,

Dm7 |G7 |B♭ |Gm7♭5 | |N.C. | ‖
Say,   hey.

Verse 3

F |B♭m6
She thinks I can't see the smile that she's faking

  |Dm7 |Cm7   F7 |
And poses for pictures that aren't   being taken.

B♭ |C   Dm |Gm7 |C   Dm |
   I loved you;   gray sweat pants,

B♭ |C   Dm |C7sus4 C7 |C7sus4 C7 ‖
   No make - up,   so per - fect.

Chorus 3

F | |Dm7 | |
   Our love was   comfort - 'ble and

B♭ | |C7sus4 |C7 |
   So broken in.

F | |Dm7 | |
   She's perfect,   so flawless.

A♭maj7 |Cm7 |Dm7 |G7 |
    I'm not im - pressed.

A♭maj7 |Cm7 |Dm7 |G7 |B♭ |C7 |
    I want you back.

F |B♭m6   C7sus4 |F |B♭m6   C7sus4 |F ‖

Daughters

Words and Music by
John Mayer

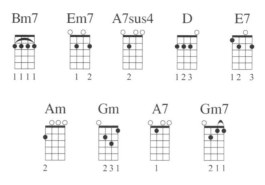

Intro

| Bm7 | Em7 | A7sus4 | D | |
| Bm7 | Em7 | A7sus4 | D | |

Verse 1

Bm7   Em7
I know a girl;

        A7sus4   D
She puts the col - or inside of my world.

  Bm7   Em7
But she's just like a maze

        A7sus4   D
Where all of the walls all continually change.

  Bm7   Em7
And I've done all I can

        A7sus4   D
To stand on her steps with my heart in my hand.

  Bm7   Em7
Now I'm starting to see

  A7sus4   D
Maybe it's got nothing to do with me.

Chorus

```
        Bm7              E7         |A7sus4  D      |
        Fathers, be good  to your daugh - ters.
        Bm7              E7              |A7sus4  D        |
        Daughters will love   like you do.
        Bm7          E7      |A7sus4              D
        Girls become lovers who turn into moth - ers.
           |Bm7              E7        |A7sus4     D          ||
        So mothers, be good   to your daughters, too.
```

Interlude 1

```
        Bm7              |Em7             |A7sus4          |D              ||
```

Verse 2

```
        Bm7              |Em7
        Oh, you see that skin?
                     |A7sus4                      |D
        It's the same        she's been standing in
                    |Bm7              |Em7
        Since the day she saw him walking away.
                    |A7sus4                      |D              ||
        Now she's left cleaning up the mess he made.      So
```

Repeat Chorus

Bridge 1

```
        Am      Gm                   |D
            Boys      you can break.
            |A7                                 |Bm7
        You'll find out how much they can take.
                            |Em7                    |D
        Boys will be strong,      and boys soldier on,
                             |Gm7
        But boys would be gone       without the warmth
             |A7        |                      ||
        From a woman's  good,  good  heart.
```

Interlude 1   **Bm7**   **E7**   **|A7sus4** **D**   **|Bm7**   **E7**   **|A7sus4** **D**

                  ‖Bm7   **E7**   **|A7sus4**

Bridge 2   On behalf of every man looking out for every girl,

D   **|Bm7**   **E7**   **|A7sus4** **D**   **‖**

You are the god and the weight of her world.   So

Repeat Chorus

       |Bm7   **E7**   **|A7sus4** **D**

So mothers, be good to your daughters, too.

       |Bm7   **E7**   **|A7sus4** **D**   **‖**

So mothers, be good to your daughters, too.

Dreaming with a Broken Heart

Words and Music by
John Mayer

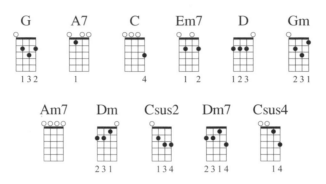

Intro   G   A7 |C |G   A7 |C ||

Verse 1
G   A7 |C |
When you're dreaming with a bro - ken heart,
G   A7 |C |
The waking up is the hardest part.
G   A7 |C |
You roll out of bed and down on your knees,
G   A7 |C
And for a moment, you can hard - ly breathe,

Chorus 1
          ||Em7 D G   C |
Wondering, was   she real - ly here?
     |Em7 D G   C |
Is she stand - ing in my room?
     |G |C G   Gm   Am7 |
No, she's not, 'cause she's gone, gone, gone,   gone,
G   A7 |C |G   A7 |C ||
Gone.

Verse 2

```
G              A7              |C            |
When you're dreaming with a bro - ken heart,
G    A7          |C          |
The giving up is the hardest part.
G    A7              |C          |
She takes you in with her crying eyes,
G          A7          |C
Then all at once you have to say goodbye.
```

Chorus 2

```
      ||Em7 D  G      C   |
Wondering, could you stay, my love?
       |Em7 D  G     C   |
And will you wake up by my side?
      |G                |C   G   Gm   Am7 |
No, she can't,      'cause she's gone, gone, gone, gone,
G    Dm   |Csus2 C  G      |      Dm7   |Csus4 C  G        ||
Gone.
```

Interlude

```
G    A7    |C              |G    A7    |C              |

G    A7    |C              |G    A7    |C
```

Bridge

```
            ||G              A7              |C
Now, do I have to fall asleep with roses in my hands?
       |G            A7              |C
Do I have to fall asleep with roses in my hands?
          |G              A7              |C
And do I have to fall asleep with ros - es in my hands?
          |G              A7              |C
Do I have to fall asleep with ros  -  es in my, ros - es in my hands?
```

Chorus 3

‖**Em7 D   G   C** |
And would you get them if I did?

|**G** |**C**   **G**   **Gm**   **Am7** |
No, you won't, 'cause she's gone, gone, gone,   gone,

G   **A7** |**C** |**G**   **A7** |**C**   ‖
Gone.

Outro

G   **A7** |**C** |
When you're dreaming with a bro - ken heart,

G   **A7** |**C**   ‖
The waking up is the hardest part.

Friends, Lovers or Nothing

Words and Music by
John Mayer

Intro   **Bm** **E7** |**D** **A** | |**B7** |**Bm7** **E7** |**D** **A** ||

Verse 1

A |**B7** |
Now that we are over as the loving kind,

Bm7   **E7** |**D**   **A** |
We'll be dreaming ways to keep the good alive.

A |**B7** |
Only when we want is not a compromise,

Bm7   **E7** |**D**   **A** ||
I'd be pouring tears into your drying eyes.

Chorus 1

F♯m |**B7** |
Friends, lovers, or nothing;

Bm7   **E7** |**A** **E** |
There can on - ly be one.

F♯m |**B7** |
Friends, lovers, or nothing;

      |**Bm7**   **E7** |**D**   **A** |
There'll nev - er be an in - between, so give it up.

A |**B7** |**Bm7** **E7** |**D** **A**

Verse 2

```
        ‖A                                        |B7
You whisper, "Come on over" 'cause you're two drinks in.
   |Bm7            E7           |D      A       |
But in the morning I  will say good - bye again.
A                                |B7
Think we'll never fall into the jealous game?
     |Bm7                    E7           |D           A      ‖
The streets will flood with blood  of those who felt the same.
```

Repeat Chorus 1

```
A           |B7          |Bm7 E7   |D   A    E   ‖
```

Chorus 2

```
F♯m                         |B7              |
   Friends, lovers, or nothing;
Bm7            E7           |A      E   |
  We can really only ever be one.
F♯m             |B7
   Friends, lovers, or nothing;
       |Bm7            E7         |D     A    |        |B7
There'll nev  -  er be an in - between, so give it up.
       |Bm7          E7       |D     A    ‖
We'll nev  -  er be the in - between, so give it up.
```

Interlude

```
A   E    |F♯m7 A7   |Dmaj7  G7sus4 G7 |A   E7         ‖
```

Outro

| A   E |F#m7   A7 |Dmaj7
   Anything other than yes is no. Anything other than stay is go.

       G7sus4   G7 |A   E7 |
Anything less than "I love you" is   ly - ing.

| A   E |F#m7   A7 |Dmaj7
   Anything other than yes is no. Anything other than stay is go.

       G7sus4   G7 |A   E7 |
Anything less than "I love you" is   ly - ing.

| A   E |F#m7   A7 |Dmaj7
   Anything other than yes is no. Anything other than stay is go.

       G7sus4   G7 |A   E7 |
Anything less than "I love you" is   ly - ing.

| A   E |F#m   A7 |Dmaj7
   Anything other than yes is no. Anything other than stay is go.

       G7sus4   G7 |A   E7 |A ||
Anything less than "I love you" is   ly - ing.

Gravity

Words and Music by
John Mayer

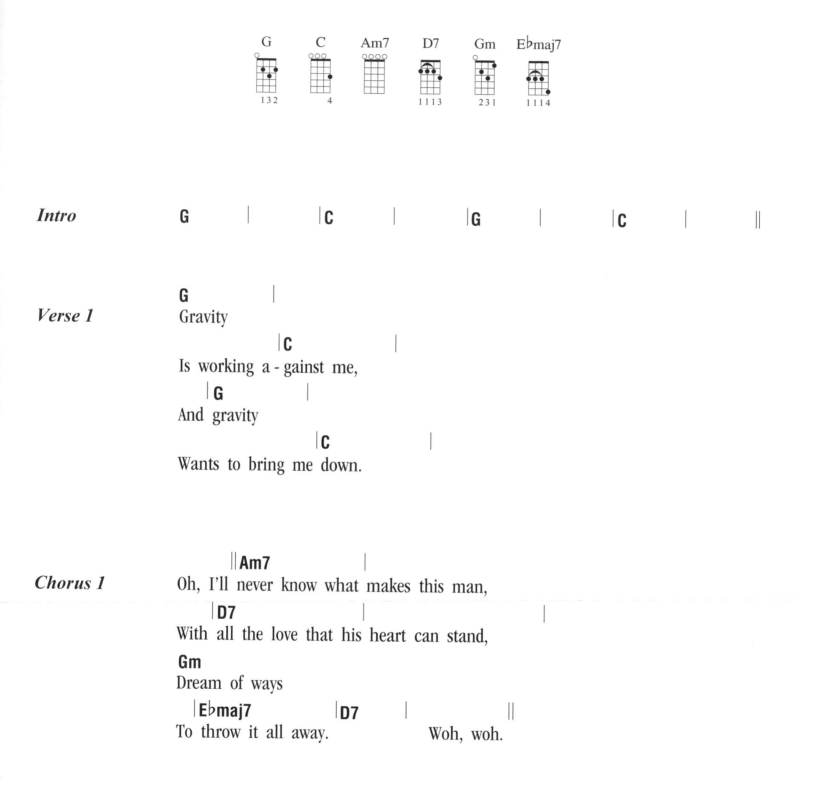

Intro G | | C | | G | | C | ||

Verse 1
G |
Gravity
|C |
Is working a - gainst me,
|G |
And gravity
|C |
Wants to bring me down.

Chorus 1
||Am7 |
Oh, I'll never know what makes this man,
|D7 | |
With all the love that his heart can stand,
Gm
Dream of ways
|Ebmaj7 |D7 | ||
To throw it all away.   Woh, woh.

Repeat Verse 1

Chorus 2

‖**Am7** |
Oh, twice as much ain't twice as good
|**D7** |
And can't sustain like one-half could.
|**Gm**
It's wanting more
|**E♭maj7** |**D7** | ‖
That's gonna send me to my knees.

Interlude **G** | |**C** | |**G** | |**C** |

Repeat Chorus 2

Verse 2

‖**G** |
Woh, woh. Gravity,
|**C** |
Stay the hell a - way from me.
|**G** |
Woh, woh. Gravity
|**C** |
Has taken better men   than me.   How can that be?

Outro

‖**G** |
Just keep me where the light is.
|**C** |
Just keep me where the light is.
|**G** |
Just keep me where the light is.
|**C** | |**G** ‖
Come on, keep me where the light is.

Half of My Heart

Words and Music by
John Mayer

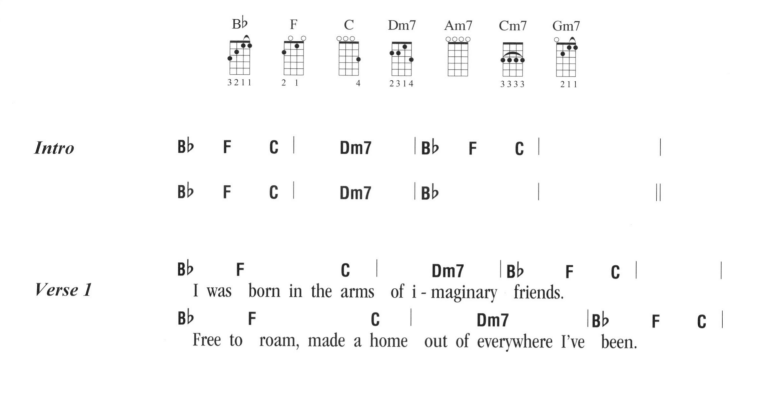

Intro

Bb   F   C | Dm7 |Bb   F   C | |

Bb   F   C | Dm7 |Bb | ‖

Verse 1

Bb   F   C | Dm7 |Bb   F   C | |
I was born in the arms of i - maginary friends.

Bb   F   C | Dm7 |Bb   F   C |
Free to roam, made a home out of everywhere I've been.

Pre-Chorus 1

‖Bb |F
Then you come on crashing in

|C |Dm7
Like the real - est thing.

|Bb |F
Try'n' my best to understand

|C |
All that your love can bring.

Chorus 1

```
  ‖Bb         F              C  |      Dm7              |
  Oh, half of my heart's got a grip   on the situation,
  Bb        F          C  |                     |
  Half of my heart takes time.
  Bb        F           C  |      Dm7            |
  Half of my heart's got a right  mind to tell you
          |Bb                  |                   |
  That I can't keep loving you (can't keep loving you),
  Bb              C              ‖
     Oh, with half of my heart.
```

Interlude

```
  F        C     |Dm7     Bb   |F       C      |Dm7     Bb      ‖
```

Verse 2

```
  Bb      F            C  |        Dm7         |Bb    F      C |            |
     I was  made to be-lieve  I'd never love somebody  else.
  Bb      F            C  |        Dm7         |Bb    F      C |
     Made a  plan, stay the man  who can only love him - self.
```

Pre-Chorus 2

```
  ‖Bb                      |F
  Lone - ly was the song I sang
             |C            |Dm7
  Till the day   you came,
          |Bb                 |F
  And show - ing me another way
                   |C          |
  And all that my love  can bring.
```

Repeat Chorus 1

```
  F       C    |Dm7        Bb        |F      C    |Dm7        Bb
            With half of my heart.
```

Bridge

```
        ‖F            |Am7
Your faith    is strong
            |Cm7               |Gm7
But I can only fall short for so long.
                    |F             |Am7
Down the road      later on,
            |Cm7                  |Gm7
You will hate that I never gave more to you
    |Bb                  |
Than half of my heart.
        |C                        |
But I can't stop loving you (I can't stop loving you).
    |Bb                   |
I can't stop loving you (I can't stop loving you).
    |C                 |                    |
I can't stop loving you  with half of my,
Bb        F    C |   Dm7 |Bb        F    C |            ‖
Half of my heart,          oh, half of my heart.
```

Chorus 2

```
Bb        F         C |        Dm7         |
Half of my heart's got a real  good imagination,
Bb        F        C |            |
Half of my heart's got you.
Bb        F         C |        Dm7
Half of my heart's got a right  mind to tell you
    |Bb        F         C|            |
That half of my heart won't do.
Bb        F        C |        Dm7
Half of my heart is a shot - gun wedding
        |Bb       F          C|
To a bride  with a paper ring.
    |Bb       F         C |        Dm7
And half of my heart is the part  of a man
            |Bb       F    C |        ‖
Who's never truly loved anything.
```

Outro

| Bb | | F | C | | Dm7 | Bb | | F | C | | | | |
Half of my heart,   oh, half of my heart.

| Bb | | F | C | | Dm7 | Bb | | F | C | | | | |
Half of my heart,   oh, half of my heart.

| Bb | | F | C | | Dm7 | Bb | | F | C | | | | |
Half of my heart,   oh, half of my heart.

| Bb | | F | C | | Dm7 | Bb | | F | C | | | F | ‖ |
Half of my heart,   oh, half of my heart.

The Heart of Life

Words and Music by
John Mayer

(Tune down one half setp; low to high: G♭-C♭-E♭-A♭)

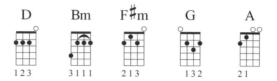

Intro   D | |Bm | |F♯m |G |D |A ||

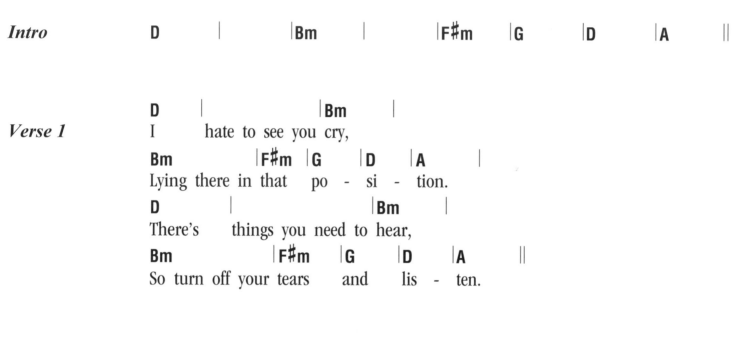

Verse 1

D | |Bm |
I   hate to see you cry,
Bm |F♯m |G |D |A |
Lying there in that   po - si - tion.
D | |Bm |
There's   things you need to hear,
Bm |F♯m |G |D |A ||
So turn off your tears   and   lis - ten.

Chorus 1

A |D |G | |
Pain throws your heart to the ground.
A |D |G | |
Love turns the whole thing a - round.
A |D |G |D
No, it won't all go the way it should,
  |G |D |A |D | ||
But I know the heart of life is good.

Repeat Intro

Verse 2

```
D                    |Bm        |
You      know, it's nothing new.
Bm           |F♯m  |G    |D    |A
Bad news never had    good    tim  -  ing.
   |D         |          |Bm        |
But then, the circle of your friends
Bm              |F♯m  |G    |D    |A        ||
Will defend the sil  -  ver    lin  -  ing.
```

Repeat Chorus 1

Repeat Intro (2x)

Chorus 2

```
A                    |D          |G      |     |
Pain throws your heart    to the ground.
A                  |D        |G      |     |
Love turns the whole    thing around.
A        |D          |G    |D
Fear is a friend who's mis - under - stood,
   |G       |D     |G    |D
But I know the heart of life is good.
   |A        |     |     ||
I know it's good.
```

Heartbreak Warfare

Words and Music by
John Mayer

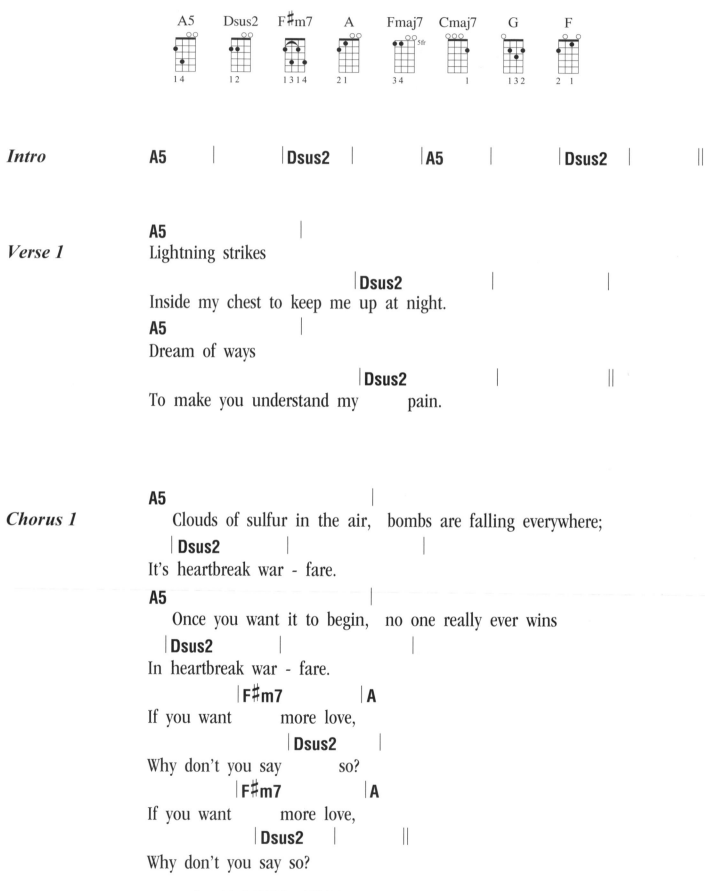

Intro   **A5** | |**Dsus2** | **A5** | |**Dsus2** | ||

Verse 1

A5 |
Lightning strikes

                    |**Dsus2** | |
Inside my chest to keep me up at night.

A5 |
Dream of ways

                |**Dsus2** | ||
To make you understand my   pain.

Chorus 1

A5 |
  Clouds of sulfur in the air, bombs are falling everywhere;

|**Dsus2** | |
It's heartbreak war - fare.

A5 |
  Once you want it to begin, no one really ever wins

|**Dsus2** | |
In heartbreak war - fare.

        |**F#m7** |**A**
If you want   more love,

            |**Dsus2** |
Why don't you say   so?

        |**F#m7** |**A**
If you want   more love,

           |**Dsus2** | ||
Why don't you say so?

Verse 2

A5
Drop his name,

                |Dsus2 | |
Push it in and twist the knife again.
A5 |
Watch my face

               |Dsus2 | ||
As I pretend to feel no   pain, pain, pain.

Repeat Chorus 1

Interlude

      ||Fmaj7 **|Cmaj7** **|Fmaj7** **|Cmaj7** |
Just say so.
Fmaj7 **|Cmaj7** **|Fmaj7** **|Cmaj7 G** ||

Bridge

F |
  How come the only way to know how high you get me
  |G | |
Is to see how far I fall?
F |
  God only knows how much I'd love you if you'd let me,
  |G |
But I can't break through it all.
      |A5 |
It's a heart,
  |A5 | ||
Heart - break.

Chorus 2

A5 |

I don't care if we don't sleep at all   tonight;

     | **Dsus2** | |

Let's just fix this whole thing now.

A5 |

I swear to God we're gonna get it right

   | **Dsus2** | |

If you lay your weapon down.

A5 |

Red wine and Ambien, you're talking shit again.

 | **Dsus2** | |

It's heartbreak war - fare.

A5 |

Good to know it's all a game. Disappointment has a name;

 | **Dsus2** | | **A5** |

It's heartbreak, heart - break.

 | **Dsus2** | | **A5** |

It's heartbreak war - fare.

 | **Dsus2** | | **A5** ||

It's heartbreak war - fare.

Love Soon

Words and Music by
John Mayer and Clay Cook

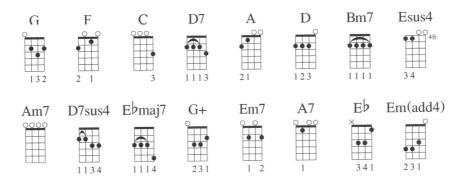

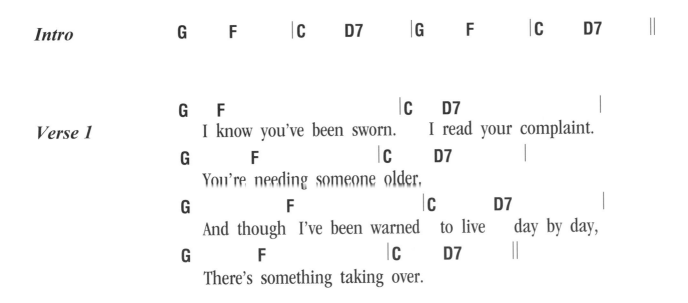

Intro   G   F |C   D7 |G   F |C   D7   ‖

Verse 1

G   F |C   D7 |
    I know you've been sworn.   I read your complaint.

G   F |C   D7 |
    You're needing someone older,

G   F |C   D7 |
    And though I've been warned   to live   day by day,

G   F |C   D7   ‖
    There's something taking over.

Pre-Chorus 1

```
       A           G          |D                    |
       Did you ex - pect to kiss me one time

       A           G          |D              Bm7    |
       While looking at me with the same eyes ever a - gain?

                   Esus4|          |Bm7
       So come on and face    it.

                   Esus4|          |Am7
       So come on and face    it.

                   Dsus4|    C   D   G   ||
       It's time that we say     it.
```

Chorus

```
       G                         D                |
       You can cross the line when - ever you want to.

       Am7           C           |
          I'm calling    it love soon.

       G                             D                  |
       Close your mind and waste some time if you have to.

       Am7           C           |
          I'm calling    it love soon.

       G       D    |Am7      C        |
       It's not  about       you now;

       Am7       D7        ||
       It's what  we are.
```

Interlude

```
       G    F      |C    D7     |G    F      |C    D7        ||
```

Verse 2

```
       G    F             |C    D7            |
       Your mother complains    that you need a man.

       G    F             |C    D7            |
       You haven't mentioned me yet.

       G    F             |C    D7            |
       And all of your friends    don't know who I am.

       G    F             |C    D7            ||
       I've been your best-kept secret.
```

40

Pre-Chorus 2

```
         A          G              |D                     |
         I under - stand I wasn't part of the plan.
         A          G              |D                    Bm7    |
         A dollar short, a minute early, but I am your man.
                     Esus4|              |Bm7
         So come on and face     it.
                     Esus4|              |Am7
         So come on and face     it.
                     D7sus4|    C   D   G  ||
         It's time that we say      it.
```

Repeat Chorus

```
         G     F        |C            D7       |G    F         |Ebmaj7              ||
                         It's what   we are.
```

Bridge

```
         G                           |G+
         Let's bypass the bullshit    and move on because
         |Em7                                    |A7                        |
         The minute hand moves faster than you think      it does.
         Am7                         |Bm7
         And by no fault of yours     and by no fault of mine,
         |Eb             F           |Eb
         The bottom line is lay - ing in the bed
                              F        |G    F        |C
         That we've been play - ing in to - night,
                     D7                |G    F     |C   D7      ||
         We've been playing in tonight.
```

Outro

```
            G     D    |F                        |G     D      |
                        I'm calling it love soon.
            F                        |
            I'm calling it love soon.
            G                             D              |
            You can cross the line when-ever you want to.
            F                    |
            I'm calling it love soon.
            G                                  D               |
            Close your mind and waste some time if you have to.
            F                    |
            I'm calling it love soon.
            G          D    |Am7      C        |
            It's not  about      you now;
            Am7        D7       |Em(add4)       ||
            It's what     we are.
```

My Stupid Mouth

Words and Music by
John Mayer

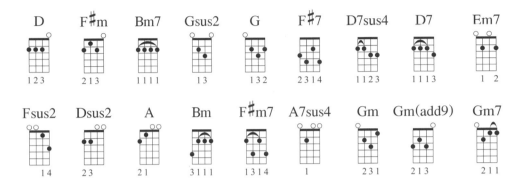

Intro   D   F#m |D   Gsus2 |Bm7   F#m |Gsus2

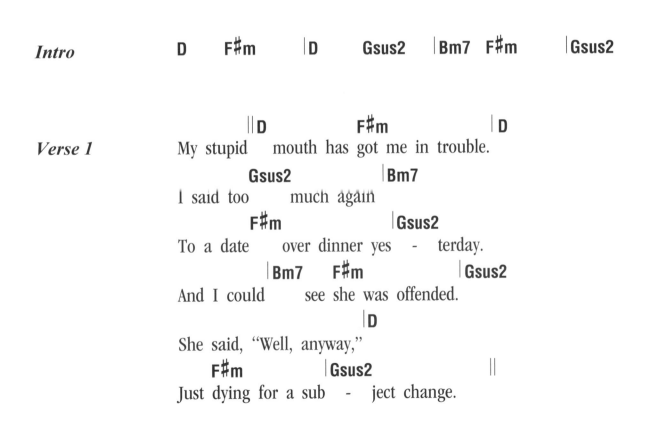

Verse 1

    ||D   F#m |D

My stupid   mouth has got me in trouble.

    Gsus2 |Bm7

I said too   much again

    F#m |Gsus2

To a date   over dinner yes - terday.

    |Bm7 F#m |Gsus2

And I could   see she was offended.

    |D

She said, "Well, anyway,"

    F#m |Gsus2 ||

Just dying for a sub - ject change.

Pre-Chorus 1

```
G                |F#7                      |Bm7                    |
Oh, it's anoth  -   er social casualty.
D7sus4   D7             |
Score one more for me.
G           D     Em7|                                    |
   How could I forget?     Mama said, "Think before speaking."
G           D              |Fsus2
   No filter   in my head. Oh, what's a boy to do?
|Gsus2                    |D     F#m        |
I guess he better find one     soon,     yeah.
D       Gsus2    |Bm7  F#m       |Gsus2
```

Verse 2

```
         ||D       F#m                  |D
We bit our lips. She looked out the window,
                        Gsus2        |Bm7
Rolling tiny balls of napkin paper.
         F#m                       |Gsus2            |Bm7
I played a quick game of chess with the salt and pepper shaker.
     F#m          |Gsus2                         |Bm7
And I could see clearly      an indelible line was drawn
            F#m
Between what     was good,
       |Gsus2                            ||
What just      slipped out, and what went wrong.
```

Pre-Chorus 2

```
            G         |F#7                                      |Bm7
    Oh, the way     she feels about me has changed.
    D7sus4          D7              |
    Thanks for playing;  try again.
    G         D      Em7 |                                        |
    How could I forget?      Mama said, "Think before speaking."
    G         D              |Fsus2
    No filter   in my head. Oh, what's a boy to do?
    |Gsus2                        ||
    I guess he better find one.
```

Chorus 1

```
    Dsus2         A         |D        Gsus2        |
    I'm nev - er speak - ing up      again.
    Bm       F#m7      |Gsus2             |
    It on - ly hurts       me.
    Bm           F#m7     |Gsus2    A7sus4       |
    I'd rath - er be       a mys - tery
    Bm           F#m7     |Gsus2        |
    Than she     desert     me.
    Gm                              |
    Oh, I'm never speaking up again,
            |D      F#m       |D      Gsus2
    Starting   now,
            |Bm7    F#m        |Gm(add9)  |              |
    Starting     now.
```

Verse 3

`‖D            F♯m                    |D`
One more   thing. Why   is it my fault?

`            Gsus2        |Bm7`
So maybe I try too hard.

`            F♯m              |Gsus2`
But it's all   because of   this desire.

`                |Bm7       F♯m          |Gsus2`
I just wanna be liked, just wanna be funny.

`                                |Bm7`
Looks like the joke's on me.

`     F♯m           |Gsus2            ‖`
So call me Captain   Backfire.

Chorus 2

`Dsus2           A            |D        Gsus2        |`
   I'm nev - er speak - ing up   again.

`Bm        F♯m7      |Gsus2              |`
   It on - ly hurts   me.

`Em7         F♯m7    |Gsus2   A7sus4       |`
   I'd rath - er be   a mys - tery

`Bm             F♯m7    |Gsus2           |`
   Than she   desert   me.

`Gm7                          Gm |                          Gm(add9)|`
Oh, I'm never speaking up a - gain, I'm never speaking up a - gain,

`                        Gm7 |`
I'm never speaking up a - gain,

`       |D      F♯m       |D       Gsus2`
Starting   now,

`       |Bm7    F♯m       |Gsus2         ‖`
Starting   now,   ah.

Neon

Words and Music by
John Mayer and Clay Cook

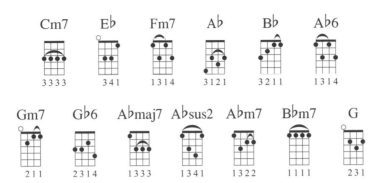

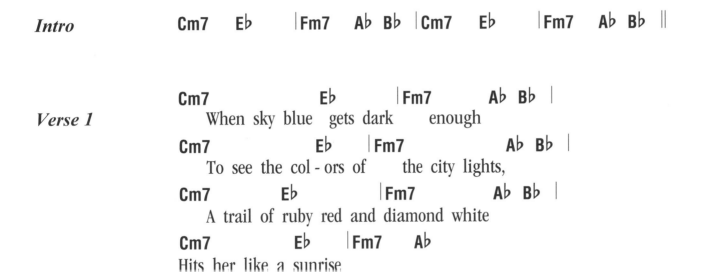

Intro   Cm7   E♭ |Fm7   A♭ B♭ |Cm7   E♭ |Fm7   A♭ B♭ ‖

Verse 1

Cm7   E♭ |Fm7   A♭ B♭ |
When sky blue   gets dark   enough

Cm7   E♭ |Fm7   A♭ B♭ |
To see the col - ors of   the city lights,

Cm7   E♭ |Fm7   A♭ B♭ |
A trail of ruby red and diamond white

Cm7   E♭ |Fm7   A♭
Hits her like a sunrise

Pre-Chorus 1

B♭   ‖A♭6   Gm7 |
She comes   and goes and comes   and goes

|G♭6 | ‖
Like no   one can.

Interlude 1   Cm7   E♭ |Fm7   A♭ B♭ |Cm7   E♭ |Fm7   A♭ B♭

Verse 2

```
 ‖Cm7                    Eb      |Fm7      Ab  Bb
To - night she's out to lose  herself
   |Cm7                 Eb      |Fm7      Ab  Bb |
And find a high on Peach - tree Street.
Cm7                       Eb           |Fm7      Ab  Bb |
     From mixed drinks to tech - no beats it's al - ways
Cm7        Eb      |Fm7      Ab
Heavy into everything.
```

Pre-Chorus 2

```
Bb          ‖Ab6              Gm7  |
She comes       and goes and comes   and goes
        |Gb6                 |
Like no    one can.
            |Ab6                 |Gm7
She comes       and goes and no     one knows
            |Fm7      Em7          |Abmaj7           |
She's slip - ping through my hands.
Abmaj7                          ‖
      She's always buzzing just like
```

Chorus 1

```
Fm7          Gm7        Cm7 |            |
     Ne - on,    ne - on,
Fm7          Gm7        Cm7 |            |
     Ne - on,    ne - on.
Fm7          Gm7        Cm7 |       Bb        |Absus2
     Who knows  how long,  how long,   how long
     |Absus2                      ‖
She can go before she burns away?
```

Interlude 2

```
Cm7     Eb     |Fm7     Ab  Bb |Cm7     Eb     |Fm7     Ab  Bb ‖
```

Verse 3

```
       Cm7              Eb          |Fm7    Ab  Bb
```
I can't be her angel now.
```
              |Cm7                  Eb            |Fm7     Ab  Bb
```
You know it's   not my place to hold her down.
```
              |Cm7            Eb      |Fm7    Ab
```
And it's hard for me to take a stand
```
          Bb     |Cm7          Eb         |Fm7    Ab
```
When I would take her any way I can.

Pre-Chorus 3

```
       Bb        ||Ab6         Gm7          |
```
She comes   and she goes
```
               |Gb6             |
```
Like no   one can.
```
               |Ab6          Gm7          |
```
She comes   and she goes;
```
               |Fm7     Gm7              |Ab
```
She's slip - ping through my hands.
```
                 Bb                 ||
```
She's always buzzing just like

Chorus 2

```
       Fm7         Gm7      Cm7 |              |
```
          Ne - on,   ne - on,
```
       Fm7         Gm7      Cm7 |              |
```
          Ne - on,   ne - on.
```
       Fm7         Gm7       Cm7 |        Bb         |Absus2
```
          Who knows how long, how long,   how long
```
       |Absus2                  |Fm7 Gm7   Abm7|  Bbm7         ||
```
She can go before she burns away,   a - way.

Interlude 3

```
       Fm7 Gm7   Abm7|  Bbm7        |Fm7 Gm7   Abm7|  Bbm7 G          |

       Cm7                    |              |              |
```

Pre-Chorus 4

        ‖**A♭6**   │**Gm7**
She comes   and she goes

       │**G♭6**   │
Like no   one can.

      │**A♭6**   │**Gm7**
She comes   and she goes;

    │**Fm7**   **Gm7**   │**A♭**
She's slip - ping through my hands.

        B♭   ‖
She's always buzzing just like

Repeat Chorus 1

Outro   **Cm7**   **E♭**   │**Fm7**   **A♭ B♭** │**Cm7**   **E♭**   │**Fm7**   **A♭ B♭** │

                Cm7   │   │   │   ‖

No Such Thing

Words and Music by
John Mayer and Clay Cook

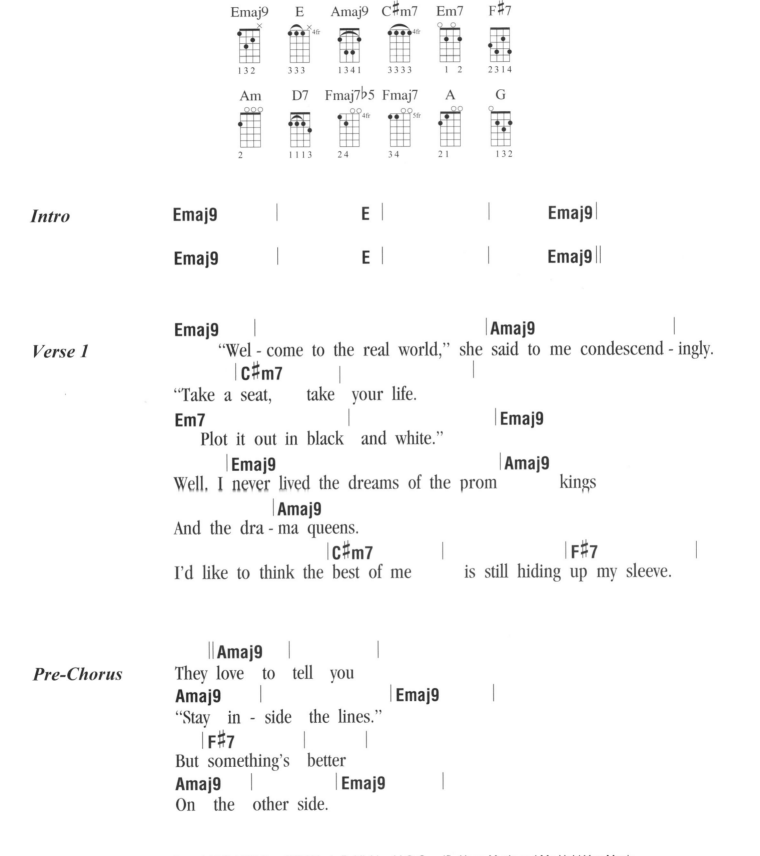

Intro

Emaj9 | E | | Emaj9|

Emaj9 | E | | Emaj9||

Verse 1

Emaj9 | |Amaj9 |
"Wel - come to the real world," she said to me condescend - ingly.

|C#m7 | |
"Take a seat, take your life.

Em7 | |Emaj9
Plot it out in black and white."

|Emaj9 |Amaj9
Well, I never lived the dreams of the prom kings

|Amaj9
And the dra - ma queens.

|C#m7 | |F#7 |
I'd like to think the best of me is still hiding up my sleeve.

Pre-Chorus

||Amaj9 | |
They love to tell you

Amaj9 | |Emaj9 |
"Stay in - side the lines."

|F#7 | |
But something's better

Amaj9 | |Emaj9 |
On the other side.

Chorus 1

```
             ‖Am                    D7        Emaj9|
I wanna run     through the halls  of my high    school.
                    |Am           D7      Emaj9|
I wanna scream     at the top of my lungs.
                       |Am                  D7          Emaj9|
I just found out     there's no such thing as the real    world,
                   |Am            D7       Emaj9|          ‖
Just a lie     you've got to rise a - bove.
```

Verse 2

```
Emaj9                  |                        |Amaj9              |
      So the good  boys and girls take the so-called right track,
Amaj9                              |C♯m7               |
Faded white hats, grabbing cred - its and maybe trans - fers.
        |Em7                          |                   |
They read all the books but they can't    find the answers.
Emaj9                       |                   |Amaj9
      And all of our par - ents, they're getting old   - er.
                   |Amaj9          |C♯m7           |
I wonder if they've wished for anything better,
              |C♯m7          |F♯7          |
While in their memorys, tiny tragedies.
```

Repeat Pre-Chorus

Repeat Chorus 1

Bridge

```
        Fmaj7♭5       Fmaj7|      Fmaj7♭5     |A            Fmaj7♭5 |
```

```
             |A             Fmaj7♭5 |
I am invin - cible.
             |A             Fmaj7♭5 |
I am invin - cible.
             |A      |G          |          ‖
I am invin - cible as long   as   I'm   alive.
```

Interlude   **Amaj9** | | | |

Emaj9 | |**F♯7** | |**A** |

Repeat Chorus 1

Chorus 2
             ‖**Am**   **D7**   **Emaj9**|
I just can't   wait till my ten - year re - un - ion.
          |**Am**   **D7**   **Emaj9**|
I'm gonna bust   down the double doors.
            |**Am**   **D7**   **Emaj9**|
And when I stand   on these tables be - fore you,
           |**Am**   **D7** |**Emaj9** | | | |
You will know   what all this time was   for.
Emaj9 | | | ‖

Say

Words and Music by
John Mayer

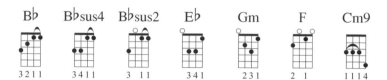

Intro |: Bb   Bbsus4 | Bb   Bbsus2 | Bb   Bbsus4 | Bb   Bbsus2

Verse 1
‖Bb   Bbsus4 | Bb   Bbsus2
Take all of your wasted hon - or,
|Bb   Bbsus4 | Bb   Bbsus2
Every little past frustra - tion.
|Bb   Bbsus4 | Bb   Bbsus2
Take all your so-called prob - lems,
|Bb   Bbsus4 | Bb   Bbsus2
Better put 'em in quota - tions.

Chorus 1
‖Bb   Eb |Gm   F
Say what you need to say. Say what you need to say.
|Bb   Eb |Gm   F
Say what you need to say. Say what you need to say.
|Bb   Eb |Gm   F
Say what you need to say. Say what you need to say.
|Bb   Eb |Gm   F   ‖
Say what you need to say. Say what you need to say.

Interlude Bb   Bbsus4 | Bb   Bbsus2

Verse 2

```
             ‖Bb        Eb  |Gm        F
```
Walking like a one-man army,
```
                  |Bb        Eb     |Gm        F
```
Fighting with the shadows in your head.
```
                 |Bb        Eb  |Gm        F
```
Living out the same old moment,
```
                  |Bb        Eb     |Gm              F
```
Knowing you'd be better off instead.   If you could on - ly

Repeat Chorus 1

Bridge

```
Cm9              |Bb          F           |
```
   Have no fear   for giving in.
```
Cm9              |Bb          F           |
```
   Have no fear   for giving over.
```
Cm9                  |Bb          F
```
   You'd better know   that in the end
```
                 |Bb
```
It's better to say   too much
```
             |F                        |Bb    Bbsus4 |Bb    Bbsus2
```
Than never to say   what you need to say again.

Verse 3

```
             ‖Bb          Eb  |Gm        F
```
Even if your hands are shak - ing
```
         |Bb        Eb  |Gm        F
```
And your faith is bro - ken;
```
           |Bb        Eb  |Gm        F
```
Even as the eyes are clos - ing,
```
             |Bb        Eb  |Gm        Eb
```
Do it with a heart wide o - pen.

55

Chorus 2

	‖Gm	B♭		|E♭

Say what you need   to say. Say what you need   to say.

	|Gm	B♭		|E♭

Say what you need   to say. Say what you need   to say.

	|Gm	B♭		|E♭

Say what you need   to say. Say what you need   to say.

	|Gm	B♭		|E♭

Say what you need   to say. Say what you need   to say.

	|Gm	B♭		|E♭

Say what you need   to say. Say what you need   to say.

	|Gm	B♭		|E♭

Say what you need   to say. Say what you need   to say.

	|Gm	B♭		|E♭

Say what you need   to say. Say what you need   to say.

	|Gm	B♭		|E♭

Say what you need   to say. Say what you need   to say.

	|Gm	B♭		|E♭		|B♭	‖

Say what you need   to say. Say what you need   to say.

Slow Dancing in a Burning Room

Words and Music by
John Mayer

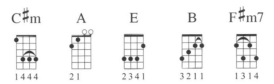

Intro

C#m | A   E | C#m | A   E |

C#m | A   E | C#m | A   E

Verse 1

‖C#m
It's not a silly little moment.
|A   E
It's not the storm before the calm.
|C#m
This is the deep and dying breath of
|A   E
This love that we've been working on.
|C#m
Can't seem to hold you like I want to
|A   E
So I can feel you in my arms.
|C#m
Nobody's gonna come and save you.
|A   E
We pulled too many false alarms.

Chorus

```
             ‖B
We're going  down,
        |C#m      A
And you can see it, too.
             |B
We're going  down,
        |C#m              F#m7
And you know that we're doomed.
        |C#m                    |A      E      |
My dear,    we're slow dancing in a burning room.
C#m              |A      E         |C#m          |A      E
```

Verse 2

```
             ‖C#m
I was the one you always dreamed of.
             |A            E
You were the one I tried to draw.
             |C#m
How dare you say it's nothing to me?
                 |A          E
Baby, you're the only light I ever saw.
             |C#m
I'll make the most of all the sadness.
             |A              E
You'll be a bitch because you can.
             |C#m
You try to hit me just to hurt me so you leave me feeling dirty,
             |A          E
'Cause you can't under - stand.
```

Repeat Chorus

Bridge

```
||F#m7        C#m                    |B        F#m7
```
Go cry about it,   why don't you?
```
 |F#m7        C#m                    |B        F#m7
```
Go cry about it,   why don't you?
```
 |F#m7        C#m                    |B        A
```
Go cry about it,   why don't you?
```
       |C#m                     |A        E        ||
```
My dear,   we're slow dancing in a burning room.

Interlude

```
C#m              |A     E      |C#m              |A     E           |

C#m              |A     E      |C#m              |A     E
```


Outro

```
                              ||C#m
```
Don't you think we oughta know by now?
```
                                |A                    E
```
Don't you think we should have learned somehow?
```
                           |C#m
```
Don't you think we oughta know by now?
```
                                |A                    E
```
Don't you think we should have learned somehow?
```
                           |C#m
```
Don't you think we oughta know by now?
```
                                |A                    E           ||
```
Don't you think we should have learned somehow?

Victoria

Words and Music by
John Mayer

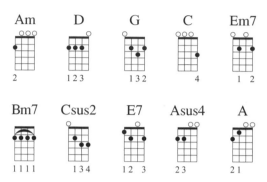

Verse 1

Am   D |G   C G |
Don't know why   Tori came by,

Am   D |G   C G |
But I could see by the look in her eyes

Am   D |G   C G |
Tori'd been driving 'round the town for a while,

Am   D |G ||
Playing with the thought of leav - ing.

Verse 2

Am   D |G   C G |
Don't know why, but Tori just smiled

Am   D |G   C G |
And mentioned something about how you were right.

Am   D |G   C G |D
It must have been hard to see through the tears   she was hid - ing.

Pre-Chorus 1

‖Em7   Bm7 Csus2 |
She said, "I might not be see‑ing him soon.

   |Em7   Bm7 Csus2 | ‖
I've got a few things I've been wait‑ing to do."

Chorus

D E7 |G   D |
 Hey,   Tori came by,

G   D |Asus4 A |
Tori came by tonight.

D E7 |G   D |
 Hey,   Tori came by.

G   D |Asus4 A   ‖
She says to say goodbye.

Verse 3

Am   D |G   C G |
 Looked outside at the car in the drive

Am   D |G   C G |
 And the suitcase on the back seat inside;

Am   D |G   C G |D   ‖
 Sure, it's so she can't look out behind at the road.

Pre-Chorus 2

Em7   Bm7 Csus2 |
 She said, "I might not be seeing him soon.

  |Em7   Bm7 Csus2 | ‖
I got a few things I've been wait‑ing to do."

Repeat Chorus

Interlude   Am   D |G   C G |Am   D |G   C G |

                Am   D |G   C G |D |

                Em7   Bm7 Csus2| |Em7   Bm7 Csus2| ||

Verse 4

Am   D |G   C G |
Don't look down;   she seemed all right.

Am   D |G   C G |
You might be asking, "Where is Tori tonight?"

Am   D |G   C   G |D ||
Somewhere out on the highway; I'm sure that she's fine.

Vultures

Words and Music by
John Mayer, Pino Paladino and Steven Jordan

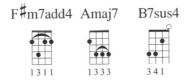

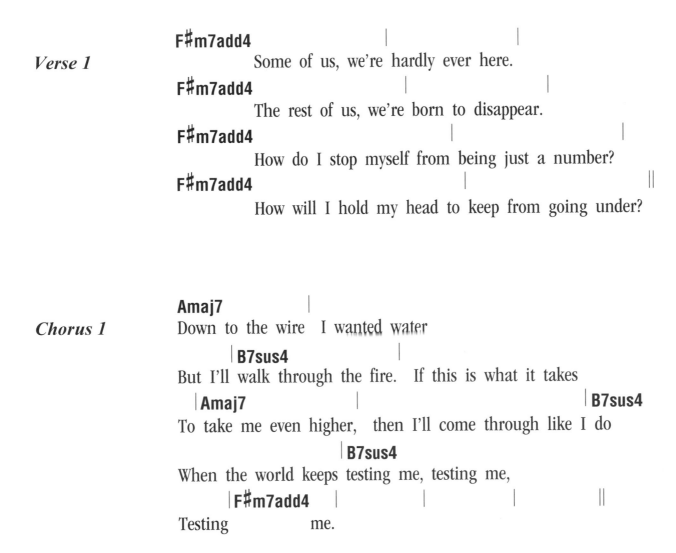

Verse 1

F#m7add4
Some of us, we're hardly ever here.

F#m7add4
The rest of us, we're born to disappear.

F#m7add4
How do I stop myself from being just a number?

F#m7add4
How will I hold my head to keep from going under?

Chorus 1

Amaj7
Down to the wire   I wanted water

|**B7sus4**
But I'll walk through the fire. If this is what it takes

|**Amaj7** |**B7sus4**
To take me even higher,   then I'll come through like I do

|**B7sus4**
When the world keeps testing me, testing me,

|**F#m7add4**
Testing   me.

Verse 2

F#m7add4 | | |
How did they find me here? What do they want from me?

F#m7add4 | |
All of these vultures hiding right outside my door,

F#m7add4 | |
I hear them whispering. They're trying to ride it out.

F#m7add4 | ||
They've never gone this long with‑out a kill before.

Repeat Chorus 1

Interlude 1

F#m7add4 | | | | | | | |

Amaj7 | |F#m7add4 | |Amaj7 | |F#m7add4 | ||

Verse 3

F#m7add4 | |
Wheels up, I got to leave this evening.

F#m7add4 | |
I can't seem to shake these vultures off of my trail.

F#m7add4 | |
Power is made by power being taken.

F#m7add4 | ||
So I keep on running to pro‑tect my situation.

Chorus 2

Amaj7 |
Down to the wire I wanted water

|B7sus4 |
But I'll walk through the fire. If this is what it takes

|Amaj7 | |B7sus4
To take me even higher, then I'll come through like I do

|B7sus4 ||
When the world keeps testing me, testing me.

Interlude 2

Amaj7 | |B7sus4 | |

Whoo,   whoo.

Amaj7 | |B7sus4 | ||

Whoo,   whoo.

Outro

F#m7add4 | |

What you gonna do about it? What you gonna do about it?

F#m7add4 | | | | |

What you gonna do about it?

|F#m7add4 |

Don't   give up, give up.

|F#m7add4 |

Don't   give up, give up, give up.

|F#m7add4 |

Don't   give up, give up.

|F#m7add4 | ||

Don't   give up, give up, give up.

Waiting on the World to Change

Words and Music by
John Mayer

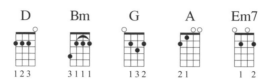

Intro

    D   Bm |G   D |A   Bm |G   D ||

Verse 1

    D   Bm |G   D
Me and all my friends, we're all misunder - stood.

  |A   Bm |G   D
They say we stand for nothing and there's no way we ever could.

        |D   Bm
Now we see everything that's going wrong

  |G   D
With the world and those who lead it.

   |A   Bm |G   D
We just feel like we don't have the means to rise above and beat it.

Chorus 1

   ||D   Bm |G   D
So we keep waiting (waiting), waiting on the world to change.

  |A   Bm |G   D
We keep on waiting (waiting), waiting on the world to change.

 |D   Em7 |Bm   Em7
It's hard to beat the system when we're standing at a distance.

  |A   Bm |G   D
So we keep waiting (waiting), waiting on the world to change.

Verse 2

```
      ‖D                  Bm                    |G            D
```
Now, if we had the power to bring our neigh‑bors home from war,
```
                 |A          Bm              |G            D
```
They would have never missed a Christmas; no more ribbons on their door.
```
                 |D          Bm              |G            D
```
And when you trust your tele‑vision, what you get is what you got.
```
                 |A          Bm              |G            D
```
'Cause when they own the infor‑mation, oh, they can bend it all they want.

Chorus 2

```
                 ‖D  Bm                       |G            D
```
That's why we're wait‑ing (waiting), waiting on the world to change.
```
          |A          Bm              |G            D
```
We keep on waiting (waiting), waiting on the world to change.
```
      |D              Em7            |Bm              Em7
```
It's not that we don't care; we just know   that the fight ain't   fair.
```
          |A          Bm              |G            D
```
So we keep on waiting (waiting), waiting on the world to change.

Chorus 3

```
                 ‖D          Bm              |G            D
```
And we're still waiting (waiting), waiting on the world to change.
```
          |A          Bm              |G            D
```
We keep on waiting (waiting), waiting on the world to change.
```
      |D              Em7            |Bm              Em7
```
One day our gener‑ation is gonna rule the popu‑lation.
```
          |A          Bm              |G            D
```
So we keep on waiting (waiting), waiting on the world to change.

Outro

```
               ‖A      Bm                      |G              D
```
I know we keep on waiting (waiting), waiting on the world to change.
```
               |A      Bm                      |G          D
```
We keep on waiting (waiting), we're waiting on the world to change.
```
               |G          D
```
Waiting on the world to change.
```
               |G          D
```
Waiting on the world to change.
```
               |G          D      ‖
```
Waiting on the world to change.

Who Says

Words and Music by
John Mayer

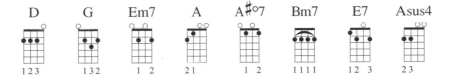

Verse 1

D |G   D |
Who says I can't get stoned,

Em7 |A   A#°7 |
Turn off the lights and the telephone?

Bm7 |E7
Me in my house alone.

 |G   A |D | ||
Who says I can't get stoned?

Verse 2

D |G   D |
Who says I can't be free   from

Em7 |A   A#°7 |
All of the things that I used to be?

Bm7 |E7
Rewrite my history.

 |G   A |D |
Who says I can't be free?

Chorus 1

‖G　　　|D　　　　　|A　　　　　|

It's been a long　night　in New York City.

　　　　　　|G　　　|D　　　　　　|A　　　　|　　　　|

It's been a long　night　in Baton Rouge.

G　　　　　　|D　　　|A♯○7　　　　|Bm7

I don't remem - ber you looking any better.

　|Em7　　　|　　　　　　|A　Asus4　|　　　‖

But then again, I don't remember you.

Verse 3

D　　　　　　|G　　　D　　|

　Who says I can't　get stoned,

Em7　　　　　　|A　　　A♯○7　　|

Call up a girl that I used to know?

Bm7　　　　　|E7

　　Fake love for an hour or so.

　|G　　A　|D　　|　　‖

Who　says I can't get stoned?

Verse 4

D　　　　　　|G　　　D　　|

　Who says I can't　take time,

Em7　　　　　　　|A　　　A♯○7　　|

Meet all the girls in the county line?

Bm7　　　　　|E7

Wait on fate to send　a sign.

　|G　　A　|D　　|

Who　says I can't take time?

Chorus 2

```
          ‖G        |D             |A              |
It's been a long   night   in New York City.
          |G        |D             |A          |              |
It's been a long   night   in Austin, too.
G           |D         |A♯°7         |Bm7
    I don't remem - ber you looking any better.
    |Em7          |                   |A    Asus4 |          ‖
But then again, I don't remember you.
```

Verse 5

```
D                 |G        D        |
   Who says I can't  get stoned,
Em7                     |A          A♯°7       |
     Plan a trip to Ja - pan alone?
Bm7                     |E7
   Doesn't matter if I even go.
   |G      A     |D           |          |          |
Who   says I can't get stoned?
```

Chorus 3

```
          ‖G        |D             |A          |
It's been a long   night   in New York City.
          |G        |D                 |A          |              |
It's been a long   time    since twenty-two.
G              |D         |A♯°7          |Bm7
    I don't remem - ber you looking any better.
    |Em7          |                 |A     Asus4         |              |
But then again, I don't remember, don't re - member you.
G            |Asus4 A    |D           |G          |

D            |G          |D          |G          |D    ‖
```

Why Georgia

Words and Music by
John Mayer

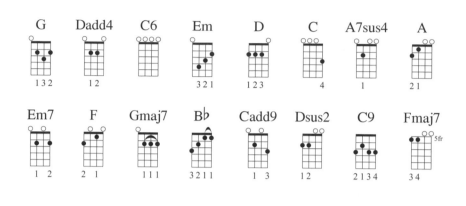

Intro   G   Dadd4 |G   Dadd4 |G   Dadd4 |G   Dadd4 ‖

Verse 1

G   Dadd4 |G   Dadd4 |
I am driving up   Eighty-five in the

G   Dadd4 |G   Dadd4 |C6 |
Kind of morning that   lasts all afternoon.

C6 |G   Dadd4 |G   Dadd4 |
I'm just stuck inside the gloom.

G   Dadd4 |G   Dadd4 |
Four more exits to   my a - partment, but

G   Dadd4 |G   Dadd4 |C6 |
I am tempted to   keep the car in drive

C6 |G   Dadd4 |G   Dadd4 ‖
And leave it all behind.   Because I

Pre-Chorus

Em |D |G
Won - der sometimes

|C |Em
About the out - come   of a still

|D |G   A7sus4
Ver - dictless life.

Chorus 1

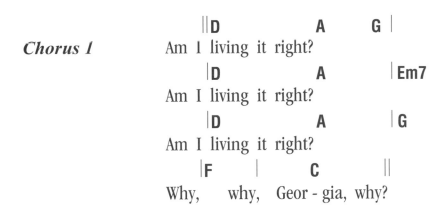

    ‖**D**   **A**   **G** |
Am I living it right?

    |**D**   **A** |**Em7**
Am I living it right?

    |**D**   **A** |**G**
Am I living it right?

    |**F** | **C**   ‖
Why,   why, Geor - gia, why?

Repeat Intro

Verse 2

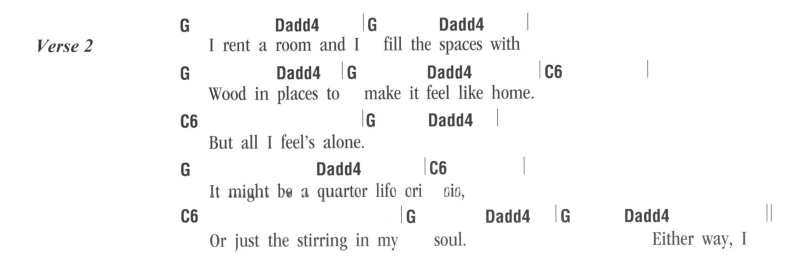

G   **Dadd4** |**G**   **Dadd4** |
I rent a room and I   fill the spaces with

G   **Dadd4** |**G**   **Dadd4** |**C6**
Wood in places to   make it feel like home.

C6 |**G**   **Dadd4** |
But all I feel's alone.

G   **Dadd4** |**C6**
It might be a quarter life cri sis,

C6 |**G**   **Dadd4** |**G**   **Dadd4**   ‖
Or just the stirring in my   soul.   Either way, I

Repeat Pre-Chorus

Repeat Chorus

G |**Gmaj7**   **G**   ‖

Bridge

F   Bb |
So what,   so I've

C   Bb |
Got a smile   on,

F   Bb
But it's hid - ing

     |C   Bb |
The qui - et supersti - tions in my head.

G   Cadd9 |Dadd4 Cadd9 |
Don't be - lieve me,

G   Cadd9 |Dadd4 Cadd9
Don't be - lieve me

   |Em7 Dsus2 C9 | F ||
When I say I've   got   it down.

Repeat Intro

Verse3

G   Dadd4 |G   Dadd4 |
Every - body is just a stranger, but

G   Dadd4 |G   Dadd4 |C6 |
That's the danger in going my own way.

C6 |G   Dadd4 |G   Dadd4
I guess it's the price I have to pay, yeah, yeah.

  |Em |D |G
Still "Everything hap - pens for a rea - son"

  |A7sus4 |
Is no rea - son not to ask myself

Chorus 2

     ‖**D**   **A** **G** |
If I'm living it right.

     |**D**   **A** |**Em7**
Am I living it right?

     |**D**   **A** |**G**
Am I living it right?

     |**F** **Fmaj7**
Why,

      |**F** **Fmaj7**
Tell me why,

    |**F** **Fmaj7**
Why,

    |**F** **C** |**G**   ‖
Why, Geor - gia, why?

Your Body Is a Wonderland

Words and Music by
John Mayer

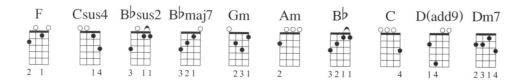

Intro

F   Csus4 |B♭sus2 Csus4 |F   Csus4 |B♭sus2 Csus4 ||

Verse 1

F   Csus4 |B♭sus2   Csus4 |
We got   the af - ternoon.

F   Csus4 |B♭sus2   Csus4 |
You got   this room   for two.

F   Csus4 |B♭sus2   Csus4
One thing   I've left to do:

|F   Csus4 |B♭sus2   Csus4 ||
Dis - cover me dis - covering you.

Verse 2

F   Csus4 |B♭sus2   Csus4 |
One mile   to ev - 'ry inch   of

F   Csus4 |B♭sus2   Csus4 |
Your skin,   like por - celain.

F   Csus4 |B♭sus2   Csus4
One pair   of can - dy lips   and

|F   Csus4 |B♭sus2   Csus4
Your bubblegum tongue.

Pre-Chorus 1

‖B♭maj7
And if you want   love,

|Csus4
We'll make   it.

|B♭maj7
Swimming a deep   sea

|Csus4
Of blan - kets.

|B♭maj7
Take all your big   plans

|Csus4
And break   'em.

|Gm   Am |B♭
This is bound   to be awhile.

Chorus 1

C   ‖F   Csus4 |B♭sus2
Your body is a won - derland.

Csus4 |F   Csus4 |B♭sus2
Your body is a won - der. I'll use   my hands.

Csus4 |F   Csus4 |B♭sus2   Csus4 ‖
Your body is a won - derland.

Verse 3

F   Csus4 |B♭sus2   Csus4 |
Something 'bout the way the hair   falls in your face.

F   Csus4 |B♭sus2   Csus4 |
I love the shape you take when crawl - ing towards the pillowcase.

F   Csus4 |B♭sus2   Csus4
You tell me where to go and   though I might leave   to find it,

|F   Csus4 |B♭sus2   Csus4   ‖
I'll never let your head hit the bed   without my hand   behind it.

B♭maj7

Pre-Chorus 2   You want love?

            |Csus4

We'll make   it.

              |B♭maj7

Swimming a deep   sea

       |Csus4

Of blan   -   kets.

             |B♭maj7

Take all your big   plans

       |Csus4

And break   'em.

          |Gm   **Am**   **|B♭**

This is bound   to be awhile.

Repeat Chorus 1

       Dm(add9) | | |

Bridge   Damn, baby.

Dm(add9) |

       You frustrate me.

       |Dm(add9) |

I know you're mine, all mine, all mine,

          |Dm(add9) ||

But you look   so good, it hurts sometimes.

Interlude   **Dm(add9)** | | | |

                  Dm(add9) | | | |

                  Dm7 | | |

```
                              ‖F        Csus4   |B♭sus2
```
Your body is a won - derland.
```
          Csus4         |F           Csus4        |B♭sus2
```
Your body is a won - der. I'll use   my hands.
```
          Csus4         |F       Csus4  |B♭sus2
```
Your body is a won - derland.
```
          Csus4         |F       Csus4  |B♭sus2 Csus4   ‖
```
Your body is a won - derland.

Outro

```
      F                    Csus4            |
```
  Da da da,   da da da da da,
```
B♭sus2            Csus4         |
```
  Da da da,   da da da da.
```
      F                    Csus4            |
```
  Da da da,   da da da da da,
```
B♭sus2            Csus4         |
```
  Da da da,   da da da da.
```
      F                    Csus4            |
```
  Da da da,   da da da da da,
```
B♭sus2            Csus4         |
```
  Da da da,   da da da da.
```
      F                    Csus4            |
```
  Da da da,   da da da da da,
```
B♭sus2            Csus4         |F          ‖
```
  Da da da,   da da da da.

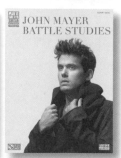